NATIVE AMERICAN
ORAL HISTORIES

TRADITIONAL
STORIES OF THE
CALIFORNIA
NATIONS

BY SAMANTHA S. BELL

CONTENT CONSULTANT
William Bauer
Associate Professor, Department of History
University of Nevada, Las Vegas

Cover image: Members of the Pomo tribe perform a
ceremonial dance in Novato, California.

Core Library

An Imprint of Abdo Publishing
abdopublishing.com

abdopublishing.com

Published by Abdo Publishing, a division of ABDO, PO Box 398166,
Minneapolis, Minnesota 55439. Copyright © 2018 by Abdo Consulting
Group, Inc. International copyrights reserved in all countries. No part of this
book may be reproduced in any form without written permission from the
publisher. Core Library™ is a trademark and logo of Abdo Publishing.

Printed in the United States of America, North Mankato, Minnesota
032017
092017

Cover Photo: Marilyn Angel Wynn/NativeStock
Interior Photos: Marilyn Angel Wynn/NativeStock, 1; Mark Ralston/AFP/Getty Images, 4–5;
iStockphoto, 6–7, 12–13, 20–21, 43; Red Line Editorial, 10, 33 (top); John Greim/LightRocket/
Getty Images, 15; Allen J. Schaben/Los Angeles Times/Getty Images, 16; Al Seib/Los Angeles
Times/Getty Images, 24–25, 45; Douglas C. Pizac/AP Images, 26; Michaeo Fiala/Reuters/Newscom,
28–29; Luis Sinco/Los Angeles Times/Getty Images, 33; Cheriss May/NurPhoto/Getty Images,
34–35; Sean Gallup/Getty Images News/Getty Images, 38; Bryan Chan/Los Angeles Times/Getty
Images, 40

Editor: Arnold Ringstad
Imprint Designer: Maggie Villaume
Series Design Direction: Ryan Gale

Publisher's Cataloging-in-Publication Data

Names: Bell, Samantha S., author.
Title: Traditional stories of the California nations / by Samantha S. Bell.
Description: Minneapolis, MN : Abdo Publishing, 2018. | Series: Native American
    oral histories | Includes bibliographical references and index.
Identifiers: LCCN 2017930246 | ISBN 9781532111716 (lib. bdg.) |
    ISBN 9781680789560 (ebook)
Subjects: LCSH: Indians of North America--Juvenile literature. | Indians of North
    America--Social life and customs--Juvenile literature. | Indian mythology--
    North America--Juvenile literature. | Indians of North America--Folklore--
    Juvenile literature.
Classification: DDC 979--dc23
    LC record available at http://lccn.loc.gov/2017930246

CONTENTS

CHAPTER
ONE

THE TRIBES OF CALIFORNIA

The long winter night chilled the village near the California coast. In the assembly house, families gathered around a community fire. An elderly man spoke. He began sharing familiar tales. His audience listened for hours. They heard many of their favorite traditional stories. After the elderly man was finished, the listeners gave him gifts. These storytelling traditions were hundreds of years old. They would continue for hundreds more years, extending into the present day.

The people of the California Native Nations are keeping traditional ceremonies and stories alive today.

California's diverse landscapes include deserts, mountains, and lush forests.

Long before European settlers ever came to the area, Native tribes had established more than 200 independent nations near California's mountains, deserts, and shores. The landscapes, plants, and animals differ widely between these areas. These differences have helped shape the cultures of the tribes. Many members of California's Native Nations still live in these areas today.

MAKING HOMES IN CALIFORNIA

Thousands of years ago, tribes in Northwest California, such as the Hupa (Natinixwe) and Shasta, created settlements near rivers and lagoons. They traveled by either foot or canoe. Northeast California was home to nations such as the Atsugewi and Modoc. This area was rich in salmon, acorn, and deer. Northern tribes also gathered obsidian to trade with other communities.

Central California was inhabited by tribes such as the Pomo, the Maidu, the Miwoks, and the Yokuts. Some tribes lived on the coast, while others lived on mountain slopes and in the valleys. Food was abundant in these areas. Tribe members hunted elk, antelope, deer, and rabbit. They created elaborate coiled baskets.

USEFUL AND BEAUTIFUL

Obsidian is natural glass formed from the molten magma in a volcano. It comes to Earth's surface in lava flows. When obsidian is broken, it has a razor-sharp edge. Native American tribes traditionally used obsidian for arrow points and knife blades. They also used it to make other tools, as well as decorative and ceremonial objects. Today, Native Americans continue to produce obsidian artwork and tools.

In Southern California, tribes established homes along the coast. The ocean provided plenty of food, and some villages became quite prosperous. The Chumash lived on the islands and along the shore in communities of up to 1,000 people.

Serranos (Taaqtams) and Kumeyaays lived farther inland, where they found plenty of rabbit, deer, acorns, and seeds. Some groups, such as the Tubatulabal and the Paiute tribes, settled in desert areas. Because resources were scarce, these tribes lived in smaller towns than their neighbors.

While many Native Americans still live in these same regions, others now live elsewhere in the United States. They carry their culture with them to their new homes.

TELLING STORIES

California Native Nations had oral traditions that recorded

PERSPECTIVES

TELLING STORIES, SINGING SONGS

Barbara Levy, a member of the Quechan tribe, is a modern-day storyteller. She grew up in southern California's Fort Yuma Indian Reservation. She speaks Quechan, which is part of the Yuma language family. Today, she travels to Native American cultural meetings throughout California to tell stories and sing traditional songs.

CALIFORNIA NATIONS

The tribes in California had different lifestyles depending on where they lived. How might daily life vary from region to region? How would geography, climate, and food affect a tribe's lifestyle?

the past. They told stories that were passed down from one generation to the next. The stories often included geographic landmarks, such as lakes, rivers, and mountains. The main characters could be people, animals, or natural objects that spoke, worked together, or fought with each other. Though the stories often had themes of love, courage, or deceit, they were not meant just to entertain the listener. Instead, the stories were a way of explaining the history of the tribe. They also provided lessons for future generations to follow. Earth Maker, Coyote, and Turtle are just a few of the characters in the oral histories of the California tribes. By learning about their adventures, readers can better understand the history and culture of these Native Nations.

FURTHER EVIDENCE

Chapter One introduces some of the Native American tribes of California. What was one of the main points of this chapter? What evidence is included to support this point? Read the section on California Nations in the article at the website below. Does the information on the website support the main point of the chapter? Does it present new evidence?

HISTORY CHANNEL: NATIVE AMERICAN CULTURES
abdocorelibrary.com/california-nations

CHAPTER
TWO

THE CREATION OF THE WORLD

The creation stories of many California tribes begin with Earth covered by water. The water was like a new, blank surface to work on. These stories tell how the creators formed the land and the people. Each creator had a different job, and they worked hard to form the world. The stories describe how a specific place was made for the people, and specific people were made for the place. The following story from the Konkow Maidu tribe tells about a man called Earth Maker

California's vast coastline may have inspired the role of water in many Nations' creation stories.

who worked together with Turtle to prepare the world for people.

THE STORY OF EARTH MAKER AND TURTLE

Turtle swam to the boat that Earth Maker was riding in. Earth Maker asked him if he could dive. "I'm good at diving," Turtle answered. Earth Maker explained that he was tired of living on water. He wanted to live on the land.

Earth Maker told Turtle his plan. "I'll make a rope and tie it to you. You dive to the bottom and get all the dirt you can." Turtle dove down and filled his ears and mouth with dirt. Then he

COYOTE AS CREATOR

In some California Nations' stories, Coyote is the creator of the people. He is smart and cunning, but he is also selfish. He often tries to trick the other animals to do things that will help only himself. In many stories, he provides a good example of what not to do. His actions may benefit him right away, but they always hurt him in the long run.

A work titled "Creation Story" by Maidu artist Harry Fonseca hangs at the National Museum of the American Indian in Washington, DC.

tugged on the rope. Earth Maker pulled him up. When Turtle reached the top, he only had a little dirt left in his mouth.

Earth Maker asked Turtle to dive again. He came up again with the same amount of dirt. Earth Maker flattened the dirt and put it at the back of the boat. Then Earth Maker said to Turtle, "Let us lie down and rest." When they woke up, land had appeared. The water had receded, and Turtle left to follow the water.

The ruins of ancient Maidu villages are now protected by modern Maidu people and California state park rangers.

THE MAIDU VILLAGES

In the Maidu creation story, water once covered the entire world, and Earth Maker floated in a boat on the water. Historically, the Maidu people built their villages near water. They lived along the smaller rivers that flow into the Sacramento River. They built brush-covered shelters or earth-covered pit houses. There are three main groups of Maidu. They are the Mountain Maidu, the Konkow, and the Nisenan. The Nisenan had the most villages.

Large Maidu villages had a central building called a roundhouse. Smaller villages often shared the same roundhouse. The roundhouse was about 50 feet (15 m) across and partly built into the ground. The walls were made with layers of sticks, twigs, bark, and earth. The roundhouse was the center of Maidu life. Maidus used roundhouses for special ceremonies or social events. Sometimes it was used as a place where visitors could stay. On winter nights, stories like the one about Earth Maker were told in the roundhouse.

FOOD FROM THE RIVER

When Earth Maker wanted to create land, he asked Turtle to help. Turtle had to dive deep down to get the dirt beneath the water. For the Maidu, the water was a source of food. Maidu people caught salmon and other migrating fish. Nisenans were expert fishermen and were known for their fishing nets. Fish were also speared or caught in small traps. Sometimes the people made small boats by lashing long grasses together. They also made fishing boats with hollowed-out logs.

STRAIGHT TO THE
SOURCE

Kara English (Konkow Maidu) describes the relationship between the Maidu tribe's three groups:

Our languages are all part of the Maiduan language family, but we each have our own distinct different dialects. Now our cultures are also very similar. We are culturally and linguistically very intertwined and connected. And for most of us who identify with being any form of Maidu we consider ourselves brothers and sisters and cousins. . . .

And our general practices of eating acorns, the ute, the richness of life, our food from the acorns; and our appreciation of sumi or deer, and salmon, our staples, are the very core foundation of our culture, our food sources, and what keeps bringing us back to ceremony and appreciation of our environment.

Source: "Konkow Maidu: Kara English." *California Museum.* California Museum, 2017. Web. Accessed January 24, 2017.

What's the Big Idea?
Read the paragraphs again. What do you think is the main idea expressed in the paragraphs? Find two or three details that support that idea.

A LIVING NATURAL WORLD

In the cultures of many California Native Nations, animals and people have a special bond. All parts of the physical world are seen as alive, and all of these parts can teach things to people. In many stories, some of the first beings are animal people. They are both animal and human at the same time. Sometimes characters begin as humans and later change into animals. The following Chumash story tells about a dog who was also a girl.

California's varied ecosystems are home to many types of animals.

THE STORY OF THE DOG GIRL

Once there were some very poor dog people. They were scavengers and could not find much food to eat. Many of them were children. They grew quickly, but they were thin and always hungry.

One of the girls climbed a hill. She saw people in the village below. They were playing games. They called for her to come down, but she went home instead. She told her mother what had happened. Her mother combed her hair until she was beautiful. Then her mother told her to go back to the hill.

The next day the girl returned. The people called to her again. The girl went to the village and ate the good food at the

SOAPSTONE

The Chumash honored the sea animals that were so important to their way of life. They carved the animals in soapstone. Also called steatite, soapstone is a soft stone that can easily be shaped into different things. The Chumash also used it to make bowls, pots, frying pans, ornaments, and pipes.

chief's house. She had acorns, fish, and deer meat. When she went home, she threw it up. Her mother and the other children ate it.

The girl climbed the hill again. The people called for her to come to the village, and she went. The chief's son saw the girl and fell in love. They were soon married. The girl received many beautiful things, such as a bracelet, a necklace, an otter skin apron, and a basket hat.

PERSPECTIVES
A CONTEST

In a Tubatulabal story, Coyote and Eagle were the chiefs of men, including Mountain Lion Man and Hawk Man. One day, Road Runner discovered animal women living on another mountain. Mountain Lion Man and Hawk Man married the women. Coyote planned an archery contest to determine who would hunt and who would grind acorns. Everyone was missing the target. When it was Mountain Lion Woman's turn, Coyote said, "Break, you string, break!" The string broke, and the arrow went to one side. Then Mountain Lion Man's arrow hit the center. The men became the hunters, and women would grind acorns. Both jobs were important for the tribe to survive.

People gather at a historic Chumash village for a ceremony.

But after a while, the girl went back to her old eating habit of throwing up. Her sister-in-law saw the girl and told the husband. The girl was so ashamed, she left the village and returned to her family. The family lost their human nature and became dogs.

VILLAGE CHIEFS

The Chumash lived on the mainland of central California. They also inhabited the three closest Channel Islands off the coast of southern California.

Members of the Chumash tribe hold Chumash artifacts found near Malibu, California.

Each member of the Chumash fit into a social group. The lowest group was the manual laborers. Next came the skilled crafters. Then came the chiefs, and finally the shaman priests. The chiefs were usually the richest and most powerful people in the village. In a Chumash village, women could become chiefs or priests. When a chief died, a son or daughter could inherit the position.

FROM THE SEA

Redwood trees grew north of the Chumash villages. Fallen trunks and other driftwood floated into the Santa Barbara Bay. The Chumash collected the wood to build canoes up to 30 feet (9 m) long. They made wooden planks and tied them together. Then they sealed them with tar. The Chumash used the canoes to travel up and down the coastline and to the villages on the Channel Islands. They also used them for fishing and hunting sea mammals such as whales, dolphins, seals, sea lions, and otters.

EXPLORE ONLINE

Chapter Three describes some aspects of life in a Chumash community. The website below also discusses the Chumash tribe. What information from the website is the same as the information in Chapter Three? What new information did you learn from the website?

DAILY LIFE IN A CHUMASH VILLAGE
abdocorelibrary.com/california-nations

STORIES AND CEREMONIES

California Native Nations sometimes use stories to honor all forms of life. This includes the plants and animals they have traditionally depended on, as well as the people's ancestors. Many stories were part of religious ceremonies. In the following story from the Hupa tribe, a boy brings ceremonial dances to the people.

THE BOY WHO GREW UP AT TA'K'IMILDING

There once was a boy who grew up at Ta'k'imilding. He stayed in the village's Big House and sang all the time. One day,

Cultures around the world, including the California Native Nations, use dance as part of their storytelling traditions.

his mother went to get some water. When she came back, she saw a cloud over the house. She heard singing coming from the cloud. After a while, the cloud lifted up and vanished into the sky. When she reached the house, her son was gone. She knew he was in the cloud. She told her husband what had happened, and they both cried.

Many years passed with no sign of the boy. One day, the father went hunting. He sat under a tree to rest. A young man walked up to him. The father realized it was his son. He jumped up to hug his son, but the young man stopped him. He told his father that he could not stand the scent of human beings anymore.

The son said he had gone to heaven in the cloud. There he found people dancing, and they never stopped. He had come back to tell his people how and where they should dance. He told his father about the White Deerskin Dance and the Jump Dance. "You won't ever see me," the young man said. "But I will always be watching the Jump Dance."

THE JUMP DANCE

In the story, the young man taught the people the Jump Dance. The Hupa, the Yurok, and the Karuk tribes practice this dance during the World Renewal Ceremonies every other year. The Jump Dance lasts ten days. Everyone who takes part in the ceremony must settle any disagreements they have with others. People pray, sing, and dance to ask for the world to be renewed and balanced.

DUGOUT CANOES

The Hupas made dugout canoes from the tall redwood trees of the Northwest. First, an old log was split in half with an elk antler wedge. Then the half-log was burned a little at a time. The burned area was scraped away with a cutting tool. The Hupa then used smaller tools to finish the boat.

CEDAR HOUSES

The Big House in the story was the largest and most important house in the village of Ta'k'imilding. Like other Hupa houses, it was likely made of wooden planks. Each house was built around a pit that was more than 3 feet (1 m) deep. The pit was used for sleeping and cooking. The walls of the house were only about 4 to 5 feet (1 to 1.5 m) above the ground.

The doorway of a Hupa house was a circle. It was just big enough for a person to fit through. Some people think the doorway represents the hole a woodpecker makes. Others think it is meant to help keep enemies out. It may also symbolize rebirth or a new start.

DIAGRAM OF A
HUPA HOUSE

This diagram and photo show what a traditional Hupa house looked like. Why do you think the Hupa built their houses partway into the ground?

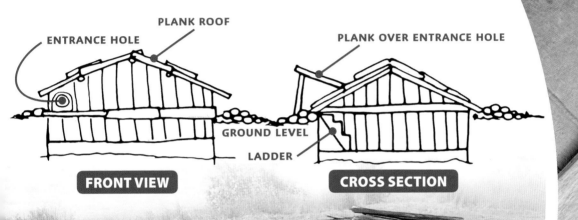

PLANK ROOF

ENTRANCE HOLE

PLANK OVER ENTRANCE HOLE

GROUND LEVEL

LADDER

FRONT VIEW

CROSS SECTION

THE WHITE HOU

WASHINGTON

TELLING THE STORIES TODAY

The oral stories of California's Native Americans are still important today. They provide listeners not just with a link to each Native Nation's past, but also hope for the Nations today. Storytellers teach their listeners how to act in the future.

PART OF THE PAST

The creation stories do more than just tell how the world was made. In the stories, the creators of the world establish boundaries between the tribes. They decide how people will be born

Jayden Lim (Pomo) was honored at the White House in 2016 for her group's efforts to share California Native Nations' cultures using modern digital tools.

and what will happen when they die. They determine how the people will be governed and the work they will do. These stories reflect a tribe's social, political, and cultural traditions.

But when Spanish settlers invaded California in the late 1700s, they forced Native Americans to make many changes. The people of the Native Nations were forced to join missions, where they worked like slaves. Stories linked them to an earlier time. Today, the stories continue to give California tribes their own cultural identities.

COLLECTING STORIES

Sam Brown is a Tribal Elder of the Viejas Band of the Kumeyaay Nation. He grew up on a reservation, making bows and arrows and sleeping under the stars. Now a retired teacher, he collects the stories that have been told by his people for generations. He tells the stories online and in presentations for students. He also enjoys sharing other historical and cultural information about the Kumeyaay.

They keep the Nations' cultures and histories alive for people today.

LOVING THE LAND

Oral histories also give these Nations a connection with the land. In 1849, thousands of US settlers invaded California to find gold. They ignored any claims the Native Nations had to the land and divided it up for farming. The tribes could no longer use the land that once provided them with deer, rabbits, acorns, and other food.

Today, only about one-fourth of all Native Americans in the United States live on tribal land. They do not always have extended families or a tribal support system nearby. Stories passed down from generation to generation can keep them connected with the land of their ancestors.

Places that are sacred to the California Native Nations are sometimes the subject of disputes. One example of this can be seen at Morro Rock. This large,

Morro Rock sits just offshore near San Luis Obispo, California.

dome-shaped rock is located near the central coast of California.

Morro Rock is a sacred place to the Salinan tribe. In one Salinan story, a giant two-headed serpent wrapped itself around the rock. It began to shake the Earth. Falcon and Raven killed the serpent, saving mankind. Today, the rock is closed to the public to protect its wildlife. But the government has given the Salinan people permission to climb the rock for religious ceremonies twice a year.

SAVING FOR THE FUTURE

Many people have been working to save stories for future generations. Some people write them down. They are worried that if the stories are not in writing, they may be completely lost one day. These stories have become part of a large collection of Native American literature.

PERSPECTIVES

THE FEUD OVER MORRO ROCK

The Salinan tribe is not the only tribe that views Morro Rock as sacred. It is also an important part of Chumash culture. In a Chumash story, the rock sits at the mouth of a magnificent river that is alive with life. The Chumash want the rock left alone. They do not want the Salinans or anyone else to climb it.

Chumash storyteller
Alan Salazar tells
a story to young
people in Ventura,
California.

Some Native Americans believe the stories are too sacred to be shared with people outside the tribe. They want to keep them within the community.

But everyone agrees the stories need to be preserved. Many elders in California are encouraging their families and tribes to tell the stories. They want their people to understand their traditions and speak their Native languages. They want to keep their culture alive through their traditional oral histories.

STRAIGHT TO THE
SOURCE

One function of storytelling is to pass on culture to the next generation. The following paragraph is a description of how April Moore, an educator from the Nisenan Maidu tribe, passed on her knowledge to her family:

My great-grandmother was Lizzie Enos, a very, very knowledgeable woman. So with her having that knowledge and carrying it on for so long, she was able to pass it on to us. Especially as a little girl, myself, my cousin, and my brother, we would spend many, many hours with my great-grandmother, where she would tell us stories about coyotes and bears and different animals. But she also took us out and showed us all the different food sources that were available to us: the grasses, the mushrooms, the berries, what kind of seeds to gather, the right kind of acorns, and what kind of herbs were outside our living area that could be gathered for our health.

Source: "The Value of Land." *American Experience: The Gold Rush*. PBS, 1997. Web. Accessed January 24, 2017.

Back It Up

The author is using evidence to support her main point. Write a paragraph discussing the main point. Include two or three pieces of evidence the author uses for support.

STORY
SUMMARIES

Earth Maker and Turtle (Konkow Maidu)

Earth Maker is riding in a boat, but he is tired of the water that covers the world. Turtle agrees to dive deep into the water and bring up some dirt from below. From the dirt, Earth Maker creates the land.

The Dog Girl (Chumash)

The dog girl and her family are scavengers. One day, the people in the village call for the dog girl to join them. When she finally comes, the chief's son sees her and falls in love. He marries her and gives her beautiful gifts. But the dog girl goes back to her old habits, and she must leave the village.

The Boy Who Grew Up at Ta'k'imilding (Hupa)

The boy lived with his parents in the Big House. He sang all the time. One day, he went away in a cloud. He returned many years later as a young man. He taught the people the White Deerskin Dance and the Jump Dance.

STOP AND
THINK

Say What?

Learning about the stories of California's Native Nations may mean reading words that you are not familiar with. Find five words in this book that are new to you. Use a dictionary to find out what they mean. Then use each word in a new sentence.

Surprise Me

Chapter One describes the diverse landscapes of California. After reading the descriptions, what two or three facts about these locations surprised you? Why?

Take a Stand

Chapter Five discusses a disagreement between Native American Nations over Morro Rock. How do you think such disputes should be solved? Should the government play a role in resolving these kinds of disagreements?

Tell the Tale

Stories can be told through spoken words, in songs, with videos, and in many other ways. Choose a story from this book and write about a way in which it could be told. Which storytelling method might be most effective for this story?

GLOSSARY

archery
the skill of shooting with a
bow and arrow

driftwood
wood floating in the water

elk
a large deer in North
America with large,
curved antlers

pit houses
a building that is dug partly
into the ground

sacred
set apart in honor of
someone, such as a god

scavengers
animals that eat things that
have already died

shaman
a person believed to have
access to the spirit world

wedge
a piece of wood or metal
with a pointed edge used to
split wood or rocks

LEARN MORE

Books

Duffield, Katy. *California History for Kids: Missions, Miners, and Moviemakers in the Golden State.* Chicago, IL: Chicago Review Press, 2012.

Indian Nations of North America. Washington, DC: National Geographic, 2010.

Yasuda, Anita. *Traditional Stories of the Northwest Coast Nations.* Minneapolis, MN: Abdo Publishing, 2018.

Websites

To learn more about Native American Oral Histories, visit **abdobooklinks.com**. These links are routinely monitored and updated to provide the most current information available.

Visit **abdocorelibrary.com** for free additional tools for teachers and students.

INDEX

About the Author

Samantha Bell lives in South Carolina with her family and lots of animals. She is the author or illustrator of more than 60 books for children.